Recycle This!

Tips on green living!

A collection of hints and tips on reusing and recycling everyday objects!

(im)PulsePaperbacks

Waste not want not!

Millions of tonnes of household waste are produced every year and the majority is land filled rather than recycled or composted. But much of this waste is not rubbish at all and is simple to recycle or turn into new products.

We are all aware that we should be recycling, reusing and repackaging to save the environment and yet there is still a great deal more we can do. We need to increase our recycling rates and reduce the amount of product that ends up in landfill.

There are lots of reasons to reduce and recycle your waste.

Landfill is harmful to the environment and expensive. As available space for landfill runs out, the cost for more space rises.

Many of the items thrown into landfill are made from products that are slowly running out or may not be replaced so quickly or easily in the future. If we use this 'waste' again, we can save space in landfill sites and reduce the need to mine new raw materials, which can damage the surrounding environment.

Many items in landfill, such as glass, will never decompose. And yet, glass is a product that can be recycled indefinitely. The use of plastic is growing every year and plastic takes hundreds of years to decompose.

The amount of packaging which is thrown away is frightening. A large percentage of your money goes on the new packaging which surrounds your new product, and this packaging ends up in the dustbin almost immediately. It is best to choose items which have minimal packaging but if you do find yourself with an item you know will not decompose easily, it is time to think 'waste not want not'!

"You must be the change you wish to see in the world."

Mahatma Gandhi (1869-1948)

In addition to reducing product waste, we can also restrict our energy wastage. We all contribute to global warming when we heat our houses or use more water than necessary. Check out our easy tips to reduce the amount of energy you use, which in turn will reduce the amount of money you spend on your utility bills.

Just following a few of the handy hints and tips in this book will help make a big difference to the environment. A few simple changes to our lifestyles can contribute to keeping the environment safe; reusing household items can save you shopping time, money and help save our planet!

Covering paper, plastics, ceramics, glass, tin, textiles, water and energy, this book will aid you in making the most of the products you already own. From practical solutions to gift ideas, this book will get you recycling and remaking!

And remember, many charities rely on reusing and recycling products to raise money. Help charities by contributing items you really cannot reuse. Always ask yourself whether your 'waste' should end up in landfill.

Paper and Cardboard

In addition to regular recycling of paper and cardboard waste in the home, there are a number of things that you can do with old paper products to reuse them.

Cards & Gift tags

You can create gift tags by simply re-using the front of birthday or christmas cards that you have received. Cut a section from the card, whatever size and shape you like, then attach to the front of a gift with tape.

Cardboard Boxes

You are probably using cardboard boxes for storage somewhere in either your house, garage or shed but here are a couple of novel ideas you may not have thought of.

Dustcover

Simply cut the flaps from all 4 sides of a cardboard box to create a handy dust protector for small appliances, keyboards, laptops etc. You can leave as is or decorate with adhesive paper or paint.

Placemats

Cut to your desired shape and cover with adhesive paper or fabric. The beauty of using cardboard as placemat protectors is that you can create extra-large mats for large oven-to-table ware and when they are worn or dirty, simply make new ones!

Tray

Create a bespoke lap-tray by removing the flaps from the top of a cardboard box and then cutting an arch in two opposite sides which will fit snugly over your legs.

Decorate the bottom of the box - which is now the top of the tray - with adhesive paper (washable is preferable in case of any spills).

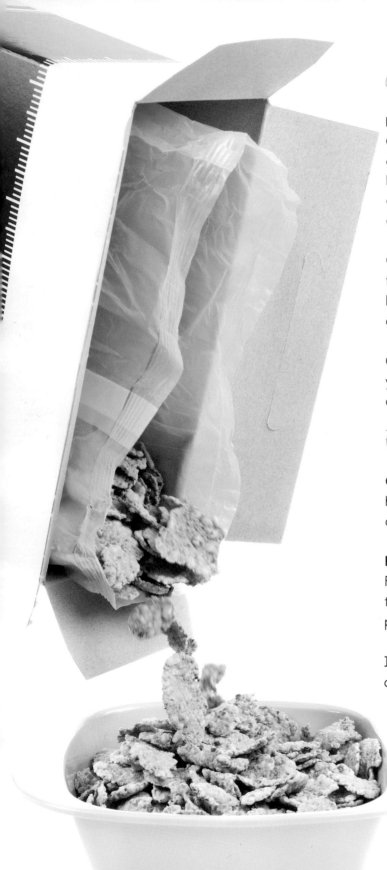

Cereal Box

Magazine tidy

Create your own bespoke magazine tidy. Measure about 10cms up from one of the bottom corners of the box, and mark then on the front of the box, draw a diagonal line from the mark to the top opposite corner of the box.

On the narrow side of the box draw a horizontal line from the mark across the width. From the end of the horizontal line, draw another diagonal line to the top opposite corner on the other wide side of the box.

Cut off the top section of the box following the lines you've drawn, then cover the box with paper or cloth of your choice to match your interior.

Egg Boxes/Egg Trays

Christmas ornament tidy

Keep glass and delicate christmas ornaments safe for another year by placing in egg boxes for storage.

Fire Starter

Fill each individual egg compartment with melted wax so that it is between one-quarter and one-half full then place a charcoal brickette in the wax.

If you are going to store this for future use, close the carton and place on a shelf. When you are ready to use, remove the top of the carton, and place the bottom half in the grill. Light the carton. Wait a few minutes and then add more charcoal. This will eliminate the need for lighter fluid.

Golf ball tidy

The base of egg boxes is great for storing golf balls!

Jewellery tidy/Little treasures storage

Keep small items of jewellery tidy by storing them in empty egg boxes. Cut the lid off the box and store in your bedside drawer. This is great for storing earrings, brooches and the like. You can, of course, decorate the box - even colour coding each individual compartment for easy use.

Seed Tray

Egg boxes make perfect seed trays - simply fill each individual compartment with the compost/potting mixture and seed.

Juice /Milk Carton

Bird feeder

Cut an entrance hole into a juice carton half way down and remove the excess cardboard so that birds can easily get inside. Push a couple of twigs or bamboo skewers into the carton underneath the entrance which the birds can perch on.

Thread a length of twine or string through the top of the carton so that you can hang it from a tree. Then fill to just below the level of the entrance with bird seed.

Desk Tidy

Cut the juice carton about half way down and cover with material or paper of your choice to create a bespoke pen tidy for your home office.

Paint holder

For small paint jobs, cut the top off a carton and clean thoroughly then pour in your desired amount of paint, which will save you having to carry a large tin.

Kitchen Roll/Toilet Roll

Christmas light tidy

Wrap your christmas lights around a cardboard tube to keep them tangle free. Push the end with the plug inside one end of the tube and work your way along the length, wrapping the lights carefully and fixing with masking tape to stop from unravelling.

Crease free linens

If you would prefer your linens to be crease free, wrap around a tube after ironing and store in a kitchen drawer.

Crease free trousers and clothes

Prevent creases from forming on trousers or other articles of clothing hung over a hanger, by slicing a kitchen roll tube along one side and then pushing over the base or rack of the hanger. Stop ugly "hanger marks" appearing on the shoulders of woolens and other clothes by cutting two tubes along one side and then pushing onto each side of the hanger. These will act as a barrier against indentations caused by the hanger.

Drawer tidy

Cut the tubes into lengths of around 3-4 inches and put in your drawers to stop items getting muddled.

Drawer tidy

Cut the tubes into lengths of around 3-4 inches and put in your drawers to stop items getting muddled.

Extension cord tidy

This works better with a kitchen roll tube and works in two ways to ensure that your cables don't get all tangled up when you are not using them. You can either wrap the extension cord around the length of the tube then put the "plug" end in the tube to secure it, or alternatively fold the extension cord back and forth in around 10 inch lengths and push inside the tube.

Fire starter "cracker"

Fill an empty roll with dried leaves in the autumn and then wrap the tube in newspaper, leaving about 4 inches at each end of the roll. Twist the ends of the paper, for easy lighting.

Nail Varnish Tidy

If you've got a drawer full of nail varnishes knocking against each other and you have to pull every one out before you get to the colour you like, try cutting tubes into lengths of around 3-4 inches. Mark the top of each piece with the colour from each bottle making it easier to identify the colour at a glance.

Paper and poster storage

Roll documents and posters tightly, and store in the tubes. Mark each tube with the contents for ease of reference.

Sapling protector

Slice a tube lengthways and place around the bottom of small trees to protect them whilst you are weeding around the area.

Seed planter

Cut into pieces around 3-4 inches in size and place on a tray. Half fill each tube with compost or potting mix and put a seed in each. When transferring the seeds, push the pieces into the ground around each seed to discourage worms and other pests.

Socks, stockings and tights storage

Fold socks, stockings and tights into the centre of tubes to keep them tidy and free from snags. This will keep them much tidier in your drawers and is also great if you are going on a trip for keeping hosiery easy to hand.

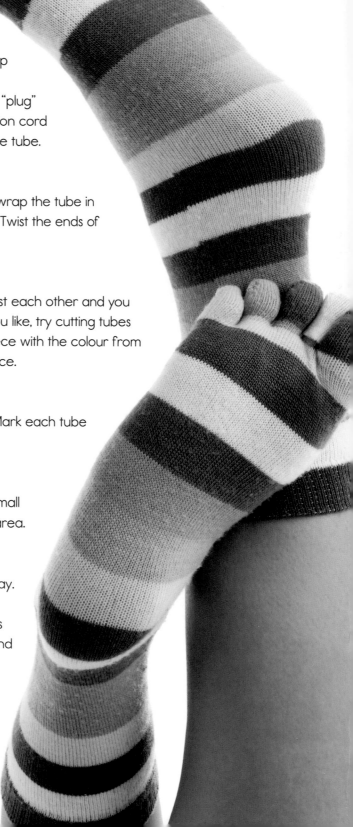

Newspaper

Newspaper, by design, is a very absorbent product, because it has to absorb ink. But that also means it is equipped to absorb all sorts of moisture.

Bird cage liner
Line the bottom of your bird cage with newspaper to make it easier to clean.

Coasters
Create your own coasters to protect surfaces by either folding or cutting sheets of old newspaper into a square. Tape the sides together to create stability and simply throw it away when it gets too stained.

Cobweb remover
Roll old newspapers together and secure around the middle and one end with an elastic band or tape. "Feather" the other end and use to remove cobwebs

Deodorize food containers
Scrunch up old newspaper and fill containers to remove lingering odours. You can also line the vegetable drawer in your fridge with newspaper to keep it dry and odour free. Refresh weekly, or more regularly in the case of spillage.

Frost Protection
Wrap fragile or small plants in newspaper in the winter months to protect from frost damage.

Kitty Litter Liner
Line the bottom of your cat's litter tray with shredded newspaper to help absorb odour.

Paper logs
Roll a few sheets of old newspapers together and stuff into the empty tubes left by toilet rolls or kitchen rolls and then use as an alternative or an addition to logs in your fireplace.

Protection from paint
When you're painting window frames or sills, wet old newspaper and completely cover the glass. Allow the paper to dry and this will act as a barrier and prevent paint getting onto the glass. When you have finished painting and the paint is dry, remove from the glass. Finish by cleaning your windows with the tip on the next page.

Ripen tomatoes
Wrap unripe tomatoes individually in newspaper and then leave at room temperature to ripen.

Shape maintainer
Scrunch up old newspapers and stuff into shoes, handbags and even hats when storing them to help maintain their shape.

Shoe dryer and deodorizer

If your shoes get soaked they can take ages to dry and develop a "mature" odour - but if you stuff your wet shoes with old newspaper, this will help them dry more quickly and absorb unpleasant pongs!

Stale odour remover

Scrunch-up old newspaper and place in suitcases for a couple of weeks to remove stale odours.

Table protector

Rather than go to the expense of buying one, create your own table protector by layering sheets of newspaper together and placing them underneath your tablecloth to act as a heat and moisture guard. You can secure the edges of the newspaper together with masking tape or decorators tape and when it is worn through, just make a new one! Much cheaper than having to re-varnish your table!

Window Cleaner

In a bucket, make a solution with equal parts water and white vinegar. Tear the old newspapers into A4 size sheets, crumple and then saturate in the cleaning solution. Squeeze any excess liquid from the newspaper then apply to your windows in a circular motion, replacing the newspaper as it begins to disintegrate. Wipe the window dry with a clean dry sheet of crumpled newspaper.

Weed suppressant

Layer newspaper around the base of your garden plants and soak with water. Spread mulch over the top and this will create a barrier to weeds, plus lock in moisture.

Wrapping

Wrap delicate items and ornaments in individual sheets of newspaper and store using crumpled newspaper to prevent damage. Do not use newspaper to store silverware.

Plastics

The world's annual consumption of plastic materials has increased from around 5 million tonnes in the 1950s to nearly 100 million tonnes today, which means that we produce and use 20 times more plastic today than we did 50 years ago. It is vitally important that whenever you can, you opt out of using plastic materials or choose wherever possible plastics that have been recycled. Choose goods with minimal packaging or in a material that can be returned to the store. Try to reduce the need to throw away plastics. Take a reusable shopping bag to the supermarket or shop, or re-use the bags you were given last time. Don't accept a bag if you don't need one. Plastic waste, such as plastic bags, often becomes litter. A study in 2003 showed that nearly 57% of litter found on UK beaches was plastic. When they are beyond reuse, plastic carrier bags can be put into collection banks at most major supermarkets and stores. Every year, an estimated 17½ billion plastic bags are given away by supermarkets, although the pressure on these giants of industry to lessen the damage to our planet, has meant the implementation of charges for bags in many stores. If you have a surplus of clean useable carrier bags, try giving these to local second hand shops, libraries, markets or charity shops who will be grateful and will reuse them.

Bags

Bathtoy collector

Hang a carrier from the taps of your bath to create storage for bath toys. Make a small hole in the bottom to allow water to drain and stop tops from going mouldy.

Biscuit basher

If your recipe needs broken biscuits, put them in a carrier bag and tie securely. Bash the bag against your work surface, or with a rolling pin, then simply untie the bag and empty into a bowl.

Boot waterproofs

Make sure that feet are kept dry in your boots or wellies. After you've put your socks on, put each foot in a carrier bag before you slip your boots on to give added waterproof protection. Alternatively, if your boots are wet when you need to put them on, put carrier bags over your feet to keep them dry.

Car tidy

Keep a handy carrier in your car to use as a bin on long trips to make sure your car doesn't end up full of rubbish.

Cracked Vase

If you have a favourite vase but it has a crack in it, place a carrier in the vase before you fill it with water which will stop any leaks.

Frost protector

If a cold night is predicted, place a carrier bag over the wing mirrors on your car and secure. In the morning your mirrors will be frost free.

Homemade manicure and pedicure

If your hands or feet are feeling dry and chapped, slather with petroleum jelly and place inside a plastic bag. Wrap a warm towel around the bag and leave for around 15 minutes which will rehydrate and soften the skin.

Litter tray liner

Line the bottom of your cat's litter tray with a carrier to make it easier to remove the used litter and clean.

Makeshift gloves

There are plenty of mucky jobs around the house - but you can keep dirt and grime off your hands by putting a carrier bag over each hand and using as "gloves". This also works if you hands are dirty and you need to touch something which is clean where you don't want to transfer the dirt.

Nappy Sacks

Don't waste money on store bought nappy sacks, simply reuse carrier bags to dispose of soiled nappies.

Paintbrush storage

Rather than clean paintbrushes when you are in the middle of a job and need to take a break, cover the brush with a carrier bag and secure around the handle with an elastic band. This way the paint will not dry on the brush and you can continue where you left off. This also works for paint rollers and paint trays.

Plant protector

As winter sets in protect your plants by cutting a small whole for ventilation in the bottom of a carrier then place the bag over the plant and weight down the handles with small rocks to stop the wind taking it.

Poop Bags

Be a responsible dog owner and carry bags with you when you are out walking to use to clean up after your pet. Take two bags - one to use as a "glove".

Ripen fruit

If your peaches or pears are rock hard, place them in a carrier bag with a ripe banana and leave for a day. The ripe fruit will release gases which will help soften the unripe fruit.

Salad spinner

Loosely wrap your washed lettuce in kitchen roll and then place in a carrier bag. Hold by the handles and spin the carrier bag quickly several times to remove the excess water.

Scrap collector

If you are having a group of family or friends over to dinner, make cleaning up easier by lining a large bowl with a carrier bag and scraping the plates straight into the bowl - this will save you having to make numerous trips to the bin. Once the bag is full tie up the handles and throw away.

Shoe and bag shaper

Scrunch up old carriers and stuff into shoes, handbags and even hats when storing them to help maintain their shape.

Stop paint splashes

Cover ceiling shades and wall lights with carrier bags when painting to protect from paint splashes. Make sure you do not switch on the lights when they are still covered.

Suitcase organiser

Use carrier bags to help organise your suitcase by putting socks in one, swimwear in another etc. You may also like to wrap your liquids individually in carrier bags to protect your clothes from leaks. Alternatively, you could just pack your toiletry bag in a carrier to act as a barrier against leaks. Carrier bags are also good for keeping dirty or wet clothes away from the other clothes in your case.

Bottles

Recently there have been many rumours and questions regarding the health risks associated with reusing plastic bottles. While plastic water and soft drink bottles are sold with the intention of single use, then recycling, they can be safely reused if cleaned and handled properly. The key is to ensure that the bottle is not damaged, has been thoroughly cleaned before each use, and is filled with clean tap water.

The reuse of bottles has recently been discussed as having possible health risks. There are two main concerns. There is a potential for the presence and growth of bacteria in these bottles, but with proper cleaning and handling, this risk can be minimised.

Another health concern sometimes mentioned around the reuse of plastic bottles is that the plastic may breakdown and release 'chemicals' into the water. Current research into this topic indicates that these concerns are unfounded.

It is important to note that water or soft drink bottles shouldn't be shared during use - they should be used by one individual only to prevent the spread of germs that can lead to illnesses such as meningococcal disease.

Refilling water bottles can result in contamination of the water with bacteria, for example from the hands or mouth of the person filling or using it.

With time and in warm conditions, bacteria can multiply to harmful levels, but safe handling and proper cleaning can help prevent this from happening.

Recent reports have specifically suggested that a common plasticiser, DEHA, can leach from plastic soft drink bottles into the liquids they hold, particularly with reuse. However, the majority of plastic water and soft drink bottles are made with a substance called PET, and do not contain DEHA. While current research indicates chemicals are not released into water by reuse, many of these bottles are manufactured to be recycled, not reused. Some plastic bottles can warp when exposed to heat in the cleaning process. It is therefore important to ensure that after the bottle has been washed in hot water and left to air dry that it is intact and has not been damaged.

Before filling bottles, wash and dry your hands thoroughly so that you don't contaminate it with bacteria. Examine the bottle to ensure that it is not damaged. After use, clean bottles and nozzles with hot, soapy water and make sure the inside of the bottle air dries completely before use. Use good quality water from a safe source.

Bottles should be used by one individual only. Don't share bottles- saliva can transfer germs that can lead to illnesses such as meningococcal disease. Make sure they are labelled with the person's name for easy identification. Again, there are of course numerous household uses for bottles, so here are just a few.

Cloche
Protect seedlings from cold or windy weather by using your empty plastic bottles to create cheap and effective cloches. In addition to protecting your plants from the elements, the bottles will also deter pests and wildlife and act as a barrier against insects and slugs.

Remove the cap and any labels from the bottle and using a serrated knife cut the bottom off the bottle. You can adapt the size of the cloche to suit your garden needs by making the cut closer to the top or the bottom, but remember you will need to push the cloche about an inch into the soil for maximum stability.

Desk Tidy
Cut a plastic bottle horizontally about halfway down and cover with decorative paper or fabric to create a handy desk tidy.

Door Stop
Fill a plastic bottle with stones to create a handy door stop. You can paint or decorate the bottle with fabric of your choice to complement your room design.

Drink Cooler
When the sun beats down and you are having a barbeque or party in the garden to ensure that you have lots of cold drinks try the following. Fill about a dozen plastic bottles with water and freeze them overnight. Put the frozen water bottles into a large bucket and add your drink cans or bottles.

The ice in the bottles will take longer to melt than if you just use normal ice cubes in the bucket and as the thawing ice is contained in the bottles it means that you can control the disposal of this, rather than have water slopping around in a bucket which could be a potential hazard.

You can also freeze smaller plastic bottles and then use these in a rucksack or picnic basket to pack around foodstuffs and drinks to keep them cool.

Extension cord tidy

As with cardboard tubes, you can make a handy extension cord tidy using the "tube" of a plastic bottle. Cut off the top and bottom to create a tube and you can either wrap the extension cord around the length of the tube then put the "plug" end in the tube to secure, or alternatively fold the extension cord back and forth in around 10 inch lengths and push inside the tube.

Piggy Bank

Decorate a bottle with paint or fabric of your choice. Cut a slit in neck of the bottle, large enough to drop coins through. When the bank is full, cut around the bottom to release your coins.

Plant and seed starter

Cut a bottle in half and fill the bottom with potting compost or soil, add seed and water. Reattach the top of the bottle (with the cap on) using tape. Keep in a warm place and wait for the seeds to germinate.

Plant Waterer

Punch a few small holes in the cap of the water bottle, fill the bottle with water and put the cap back on. Turn the bottle over and bury in the soil of your hanging basket or pot plant. Another way of doing this is to remove the cap and cut off the bottom of the bottle. Turn the bottle upside down, and set the spout into the ground or pot. Fill with water and this will allow your plants to be watered when you are going to be away for a few days.

Potpourri Holder

Cut a plastic bottle horizontally so you end up with a cup or shallow dish as required. Decorate this new container with paints, paper or fabric of your choice. Fill this with potpourri and then cover the open end with a light material that will allow air to circulate but will contain the potpourri - such as netting, lace or muslin. Use an elastic band to secure the material in place and tie a decorative ribbon over the elastic. When you need to refresh your potpourri, simply take off the ribbon and elastic band and refill.

String tidy

Keep string or wool from getting tangled. Cut off the bottom of the bottle and insert the string or wool, then pull a strand through the top of the bottle. Tape the bottom back on the bottle to keep the string inside and then when you need it simply pull the required amount through the top of the bottle - but make sure you always leave enough hanging so the end doesn't go back into the bottle.

Socks, stockings and tights storage

Cut the top and bottom from a bottle to create a tube then fold socks, stockings and tights into the centre of tube to keep them tidy. Make sure that you do not have any rough edges that could cause snags.

Containers

Many of the foods we buy these days come in plastic containers, whether they need them or not. Re-use the containers from ready meals or meat trays through your home and garden. Clean all containers thoroughly before you use them again.

Dog dish

Rinse clean a plastic container and keep it in the back of your car to create a portable water bowl.

Drawer tidy

Rinse clean a plastic container and use it to store odds and ends in your drawers. Great for storing cosmetics, nail varnishes or sewing materials.

Pest deterrent

Keep pests and slugs away from your flowers and vegetables by tempting them with a tasty treat. Dig a hole the size of the container and drop into the soil so that it is flush with ground level. Fill the container with beer to attract those pesky critters who will then fall in and meet their maker!

Seed Tray

Plastic containers make great seed trays - just wash thoroughly, fill with soil and plant seeds ready for germination.